Original title:
When We Grow

Copyright © 2024 Swan Charm
All rights reserved.

Author: Linda Leevike
ISBN HARDBACK: 978-9916-89-673-0
ISBN PAPERBACK: 978-9916-89-674-7
ISBN EBOOK: 978-9916-89-675-4

The Solstice of Spiritual Maturity

In the dawn's gentle light we rise,
Seeking truth beneath the skies.
With hearts open wide and pure,
In faith's embrace, we find the cure.

Nature whispers, a sacred song,
Guiding souls where they belong.
With every season's warm embrace,
We walk with grace in this sacred space.

The sun casts shadows long and free,
As we strive to simply be.
In the silence, wisdom grows,
A light within, the spirit glows.

Through trials faced, our spirits soar,
In the storms, we seek and explore.
With love as our guiding star,
We learn of peace, both near and far.

As night falls soft, we pause to pray,
In gratitude, we find our way.
The journey's end is not in sight,
For in our hearts, a flame of light.

Faith Under the Stars

Under the vast night sky,
Stars whisper of hope's light,
Guiding lost souls along,
In faith, we find our flight.

Each twinkle tells a tale,
Of dreams that dance and soar,
With each heartbeat, we pray,
Boundless love we explore.

The moon watches with grace,
A silent guardian near,
In the shadows we seek,
The truth that draws us clear.

Even when darkness falls,
And doubts begin to rise,
In the embrace of stars,
Faith never says goodbye.

The universe sings loud,
In harmony with our cries,
Under this sacred dome,
Hope forever shies.

Sanctuary of the Soul

Within the heart's soft shrine,
A sacred flame resides,
In silence, it ignites,
Where love and peace abide.

Wonders dwell deep inside,
In whispers of the mind,
Prayer anchors the spirit,
Leaving the pain behind.

With every sacred breath,
We draw from divinity,
In this hallowed space,
We're cradled tenderly.

The light of grace unfolds,
As shadows fade away,
In this sanctuary,
We find strength for the day.

Let the heart be the temple,
Where truth and spirit dance,
In this warm embrace,
We seize our second chance.

The Pilgrim's Embrace

On trails of dust and grace,
Each step a prayer begun,
With every mile we travel,
We seek the Holy One.

In the morning's soft glow,
Hope rises with the sun,
Every laugh, every tear,
Shares the journey we run.

The winding path may twist,
Through valleys deep and wide,
But the light of His love,
Is our faithful guide.

Through trials we will pass,
In humility we grow,
For in the pilgrim's heart,
God's presence always glows.

Embraced by sacred trust,
We journey hand in hand,
In the spirit of love,
Together we will stand.

Roots of Providence

In the soil of the heart,
Roots of love intertwine,
Watered by faith and grace,
Under the heavens, divine.

Each petal of the flower,
Sings praises to the sky,
In gratitude we rise,
Life's blessings, never shy.

Winds may bend our branches,
But the roots hold steadfast,
In every storm's embrace,
God's promises endure vast.

With seasons come the trials,
Yet, growth is never ceased,
In the garden of our souls,
God's providence is released.

Through times of joy and pain,
The harvest draws us near,
In love, we find our strength,
Planting hope amidst fear.

Pathways to Enlightenment

In stillness, sacred whispers sound,
The heart awakens, truth is found.
Each step a gift, a light to see,
The soul ascends, forever free.

With every breath, the spirit sings,
In nature's arms, our longing clings.
The stars above, a guiding hue,
In darkness' weave, the dawn breaks through.

Eternal quest, the journey's call,
To rise in love, to never fall.
With open hearts, we learn and grow,
Through trials faced, the wisdom flows.

Blossoms of Faith

In gardens lush, the blossoms bloom,
With petals soft, dispelling gloom.
Each color bright, a prayer unfolds,
In fragrant whispers, joy beholds.

The roots entwined in sacred ground,
In unity, our strength is found.
Through storms we bend, yet do not break,
In love's embrace, we rise awake.

The sun will shine, the rain will fall,
In nature's dance, we hear the call.
With every seed, a hope takes flight,
As hearts unite, we find our light.

The Tapestry of Becoming

In the loom of life, threads intertwine,
Each moment a stitch, by design.
With colors bright, and shadows cast,
A story of love, from first to last.

The fabric shared, in sacred space,
In each encounter, we find grace.
With hands outstretched, our souls entwined,
In every heart, a treasure lined.

Through trials spun, we learn to weave,
In every loss, a chance to cleave.
To rise anew, from ashes, sing,
In unity, our spirits bring.

From Seeds of Hope

In whispered dreams, the seeds are sown,
In every heart, a longing grown.
With gentle hands, we nurture soft,
The promise blooms, our spirits aloft.

In fields of light, the harvest comes,
In grateful hearts, the quiet hums.
With every tear, a river flows,
In love's embrace, our essence grows.

In moments shared, our wisdom thrives,
Through open doors, our spirit strives.
With faith to guide, the journey's grace,
From seeds of hope, we find our place.

A Dance with Eternity

In twilight's embrace, we gently sway,
Time whispers secrets in a sacred way.
Each step we take, a promise divine,
In the rhythm of grace, our spirits entwine.

Heavenly souls guide our dance so bright,
With echoes of love, we enter the light.
The ages converge in a symphonic song,
In this dance with eternity, we belong.

From Ashes to Ascension

From ashes we rise, like the dawn's first beam,
Hearts ignited, we dare to dream.
In trials we forge, our spirits take flight,
Transforming the darkness, we seek out the light.

Each tear that we shed, a seed to the ground,
In the soil of hope, our purpose is found.
From the depth of despair, we find our way,
In the arms of the Father, we choose to stay.

The Blossoming of Faith

In the quiet dawn, a flower unfolds,
The whispers of faith in each petal hold.
With roots intertwined in the earth's gentle grace,
We nurture our spirits in this sacred place.

Through storms that may come, we stand strong and tall,
In the hands of the Divine, we shall not fall.
The blossoms of love, in colors so bright,
Illuminate our path with heavenly light.

In the Garden of Our Becoming

In the garden of grace, our souls shall thrive,
With each prayer and promise, we come alive.
Hands lifted in praise, we dance with delight,
Finding strength in surrender, hearts glowing bright.

Amongst the rich soil, our dreams take root,
Nurtured by faith, we bear sacred fruit.
In this haven of peace, we bloom and we grow,
In the garden of love, God's blessings bestow.

The Eternal Cycle of Becoming

In the dawn of creation's light,
Life unfolds in pure delight.
Every breath a sacred chance,
To dance in the cosmic expanse.

Time whispers secrets on the breeze,
Guiding hearts with gentle ease.
In shadows cast by the divine,
We find our place, our spirits align.

Life and death entwine as one,
The cycle turns, a race begun.
From ashes rise the blooms anew,
In every end, a promise true.

In trials faced, in joy embraced,
The spirit grows, the soul is placed.
Each moment holds a treasure rare,
In love's embrace, we're lifted there.

So let the wheel of fate unwind,
With open hearts, we seek and find.
The sacred path that we embark,
Illuminates the endless arc.

The Divine Seed of Potential

In the silence, seeds are sown,
Within each heart, a light has grown.
Nurtured by the hands of grace,
In every soul, a holy place.

Awakened by the voice within,
We rise again, we shed our skin.
Through trials and the tests we face,
In struggle, we find our embrace.

The whispers of the stars above,
Remind us of the strength of love.
In every dream, a vision bright,
A guiding flame, a beacon light.

As rivers flow and mountains stand,
The path unfolds, the divine plan.
We nurture hope with every tear,
In faith, we conquer doubt and fear.

Embrace the gift of what could be,
In every heart, eternity.
The seed of potential, pure and free,
Flourishes in our unity.

Harmonies of the Soul's Journey

In the stillness, music sounds,
A symphony of life abounds.
Each note a step upon the way,
Guiding hearts in bright array.

From valleys low to peaks so high,
In every low, we will not die.
Together we weave our tale divine,
In love's cadence, our spirits entwine.

Through storms that shake, through light that glows,
The essence of the spirit flows.
In hardships faced, in blessings shared,
The journey reflects how much we've cared.

Each heartbeat echoes wisdom's call,
An inner dance that unites us all.
With every breath, a prayer takes flight,
In the tapestry of day and night.

So let us walk in harmony,
In laughter shared and empathy.
Together we rise, our souls align,
In the journey's song, the divine design.

The Pathway to Redemption

On winding roads of mercy's grace,
We seek the light in every place.
With heavy hearts and spirits worn,
We strive to rise, to be reborn.

In shadows deep, where hope is frail,
The gentle whispers will prevail.
Each stumble brings us close to truth,
In seeking grace, we find our youth.

Forgiveness flows like rivers wide,
It heals the soul, it turns the tide.
With every step through pain and strife,
We find the path, the gift of life.

Embrace the scars that mark our way,
For they will guide us, come what may.
In humble hearts, redemption knows,
The beauty of the love that grows.

So let us walk this holy ground,
Where grace and mercy can be found.
In every moment, let love lead,
The pathway bright, the heart's true need.

Flourishing Under the Light

In the warmth of morning rays,
The soul awakens, finds its way.
Gentle whispers guide the heart,
In His love, we take our part.

Flowers bloom beneath the sky,
Hands uplifted, we raise high.
Grace descends, our spirits soar,
Flourishing, we seek Him more.

Each beam a promise, pure and bright,
In darkened valleys, He's our light.
Hope ignites like fire's glow,
In His garden, we will grow.

Through prayers spoken, faith takes flight,
We journey forth, hearts full of might.
In His presence, burdens cease,
Finding in Him our truest peace.

Hearts united, we rejoice,
In His goodness, we find our voice.
Flourishing under love's embrace,
In every moment, seek His grace.

From Darkness, the Dawn of Growth

When shadows linger, night is near,
A seed lies hidden, calm and clear.
By grace bestowed, it takes its stand,
Unfurling roots in sacred land.

From mourning cries, the heart can rise,
With every tear, the spirit flies.
Through trials faced, our souls ignite,
From darkness birth the dawn of light.

The sun breaks through, a piercing ray,
Guiding us in the light of day.
In every struggle, strength we find,
Awakening the heart and mind.

Each step we take on sacred ground,
In silence heard, the truth abounds.
With faith that guides, we learn to grow,
From darkness bright, our spirits flow.

In the garden where we seek,
The humble find, the strong, the meek.
From despair's depths, hope takes flight,
In His love, we find our light.

Hearkening to the Sacred Call

In stillness, listen, hearts align,
The sacred call, a voice divine.
Through quietude, Spirit speaks,
In every heart, His wisdom seeks.

Prayers like incense rise and drift,
A gentle touch, the holy gift.
With open arms, we reach to Him,
In trust and love, our spirits brim.

Echoes of grace in every dawn,
Guiding us as we move on.
The sacred path, though steep and long,
In unity, we find our song.

Through trials faced, we hold Him near,
In every whisper, love appears.
The world may fade, but we stand tall,
With faithful hearts, we heed the call.

In harmony, our voices blend,
His mercy flows, our hearts to mend.
Hearkening to the sacred plea,
In every moment, we are free.

Graceful Metamorphosis

As caterpillars find their way,
In sacred grace, they learn to stay.
The promise of the sky so vast,
In stillness, shedding all the past.

Transforming shadows, light we seek,
In every whisper, soft and meek.
The heart expands, the spirit wakes,
With every choice, a journey takes.

In faith we shed our former guise,
Emerging strong, 'neath open skies.
The chrysalis of trials faced,
In love renewed, our souls embraced.

With wings of kindness, we ascend,
To realms where faith and hope will blend.
A dance of colors, bright and free,
In graceful metamorphosis, we see.

In transformation, learn and grow,
Embraced by love, we gently flow.
Each moment leads to what will be,
In His light, we find our plea.

The Pilgrimage of Self

In quiet dawn, the soul does wake,
A journey started, paths to take.
Each step a prayer, a whispered sigh,
In search of truth, the spirit flies.

Mountains high and valleys low,
In sacred silence, the seeker goes.
With every breath, a vow unfolds,
A tapestry of faith retold.

Through shadows deep and light's embrace,
We find ourselves in holy space.
With every heartbeat, echoes chime,
A melody transcending time.

In mirrored lakes, the heart reflects,
A dance of light, the spirit checks.
To know oneself is to be free,
Embracing love eternally.

At journey's end, the truth laid bare,
In unity, we find the care.
The pilgrimage leads us to see,
The sacred bond of you and me.

Unveiling Celestial Truths

Upon the mount, the heavens gleam,
A vision bright, a sacred dream.
Wisdom whispers on the breeze,
In every sigh, the heart's unease.

Stars align, their secrets beam,
In silence deep, we seek the theme.
With open hands, we dare to reach,
The light of love, the soul's true speech.

With every dawn, revelations rise,
In nature's lush, the spirit flies.
Beyond the veil, the truths appear,
In loving grace, we cast our fear.

The skies unfurl their mystic art,
In all creation, God imparts.
To gaze upon the universe,
Is to embrace the timeless verse.

In unity, we find our grace,
The divine spark in every place.
As light descends and shadows fade,
The sacred truth is gently laid.

Wings of Devotion

Upon the altar, hearts take flight,
With wings of faith, we chase the light.
Each prayer a feather, soft and bright,
In loving whispers, we'll unite.

The sacred dance, from joy to grace,
In every moment, we find our place.
With every pulse, divine connection,
In every breath, profound reflection.

Through trials faced and joy embraced,
Our spirits soar, our fears displaced.
On winds of hope, we rise anew,
A tapestry of love in view.

In depths of silence, voices sing,
The songs of angels softly ring.
Through fields of light, our souls do roam,
In faith's embrace, we find our home.

With wings of devotion, we ascend,
To realms of bliss that never end.
In love, we weave a brightened sky,
With hearts as one, we learn to fly.

The Sacred Symphony of Life

In every heartbeat, a song resounds,
A symphony of love surrounds.
With every breath, we join the tune,
In harmony beneath the moon.

The earth provides its gentle choir,
In whispers soft, we feel the fire.
With nature's pulse, we find our way,
In sacred rhythms, night and day.

The stars compose a cosmic frame,
In the dance of light, we are the same.
In unity, our voices rise,
A melody that never dies.

Through trials faced, the notes grow bold,
Each story shared, a truth retold.
In every joy, in every strife,
We hear the tune, the gift of life.

In gratitude, we raise our hands,
As one we stand on sacred lands.
The symphony, a gift divine,
In every heart, the love will shine.

Sacred Echoes of Change

In silence whispers truth and grace,
Eternal light we seek to trace.
The heart awakens, softly sings,
As hope takes flight on sacred wings.

Beneath the stars, our dreams ignite,
A journey formed in sacred night.
With trust we walk through shadowed vale,
Each step we take, the truth prevails.

The voice of love, a gentle call,
With every rise, we shall not fall.
In unity, our spirits blend,
Through change divine, we shall transcend.

Awake, arise, the dawn is near,
Embrace the path, dismiss your fear.
In every breath, the sacred bends,
A dance of life that never ends.

The Narrow Gate of Growth

Through trials faced, true strength is born,
In suffering, the heart is worn.
With weary steps, we seek to find,
The narrow gate, a path defined.

Each lesson learned, a sacred thread,
In growing pains, we sense the bread.
Of life devout, with faith we tread,
Transcending doubts, where angels led.

The path is steep, yet spirits soar,
In every tremor, we explore.
With open hearts, we give and take,
For love's embrace, the bonds we make.

In mindful grace, we find our way,
Through darkest nights, we greet the day.
Together strong, we walk in light,
The narrow gate reveals our might.

From Seed to Sanctity

In barren soil, the seed is sown,
A promise made, a life has grown.
In warmth of sun, and rains that fall,
The journey starts, we heed the call.

With tender care, the roots take hold,
Through trials faced, the heart turns bold.
Each whisper of the winds that sigh,
Brings forth the strength to reach the sky.

In bloom, we find the sacred grace,
A fragrant life, a warm embrace.
From humble seed, the spirit flies,
To touch the heavens and the skies.

Though shadows fall, and storms may rage,
The soul stands firm, it turns the page.
From seed to sanctity, we rise,
A testament of love that never dies.

The Spiritual Yearning of the Ages

In every heart, a longing grows,
A quest for truth, the spirit knows.
Across the ages, souls unite,
In endless search for sacred light.

From ancient scrolls to whispered dreams,
The thread of faith in silence gleams.
With each new dawn, the Spirit calls,
Within the heart, His love enthralls.

In every tear, a lesson learned,
In every life, the flame is burned.
With open arms, we rise to see,
The journey's grace, our destiny.

Through every doubt, a glimmer shines,
As love in kindness intertwines.
Embrace the call, the ages blend,
In spiritual yearning, we ascend.

The Anointing of Time

In the stillness of the dawn, we pray,
For the grace to guide our way.
Each moment blessed, in His light,
Awakening souls, embracing the night.

Time flows gently, a river divine,
Carrying hearts, where His love does shine.
The past may linger, shadows may cling,
Yet in His presence, hope's song we sing.

With every tick, a chance to renew,
To seek the path, and be made true.
In sacred hours, we find our voice,
In the heart of time, we rejoice.

Anoint our days, with mercy's balm,
In trials faced, we find our calm.
Let every second resound, reflect,
A journey of faith, we shall protect.

So let the clock tick with purpose anew,
For the anointing of time is our due.
In His embrace, we find our peace,
From the burdens of life, we seek release.

The Chosen Path of Our Souls

In twilight's glow, a path unfolds,
Whispers of destiny, stories untold.
Each step we take, a sacred decree,
In the dance of faith, our spirits fly free.

The mountains we climb, the valleys we tread,
With visions of light that softly spread.
In the court of silence, we feel His call,
Guiding our hearts, through shadows that fall.

We walk with purpose, hand in hand,
Bound by the love that does understand.
The map of our lives, drawn by His grace,
Leads to the promise of a heavenly place.

Each misstep counts as a lesson of gold,
In the tapestry woven, our stories unfold.
The chosen path, illuminated bright,
Moves us closer to eternal light.

With every heartbeat, we find our way,
In the arms of the Divine, we choose to stay.
The journey is holy, the promise is sure,
With every step on this path, we endure.

The Divine Whisper of Change

In the depth of night, a whisper calls,
A breath of hope, as the stillness falls.
Change begins softly, like a quiet stream,
Guiding our hearts towards a new dream.

The winds may shift, and seasons may turn,
In the face of change, our spirits learn.
The courage to bend, to stretch, to flow,
In the arms of the Divine, we gladly grow.

When darkness lingers, and shadows loom near,
The whisper of change drives away fear.
With faith as our anchor and love as our guide,
We open our hearts and let hope reside.

Miracles flourish when we embrace the new,
The beauty of change reveals what is true.
In the silence of trust, our hearts find their way,
Through the divine whispers that never betray.

So listen closely, dear soul, and see,
The gifts of change are meant to be free.
In the tapestry woven by heavenly hands,
The divine whisper of change ever stands.

Sanctified Steps Forward

With each step forward, we rise up in grace,
Our feet on the ground, our hearts in His space.
Guided by truth, we strive for the light,
Walking together, through the dark of the night.

In every footfall, His love we proclaim,
A journey of purpose, a path to His name.
Sacred our mission, blessed our way,
In the arms of the Father, we fervently pray.

The burdens we carry, we lay at His feet,
In the rhythm of faith, our souls find their beat.
With courage ignited, we dance to His song,
In the harmony of hope, where we truly belong.

Every trial faced, becomes a stepping stone,
In the garden of grace, we are never alone.
The future awaits with promise so bright,
Sanctified steps, lead us into the light.

So onward we march, hand in hand with the Divine,
In the tapestry woven, our lives intertwine.
Forever we stand, in faith we believe,
With sanctified steps, in His love we receive.

Ascendancy of the Spirit

In the quiet of the morn, we rise,
Seeking grace beneath the skies.
Hearts ablaze with holy fire,
Fingers trace the divine choir.

Whispers soft, a guiding hand,
Teaches us to understand.
In each breath, the sacred flow,
Leading forth where blessings grow.

Mountains high, we climb the steep,
Promises of faith to keep.
With each step, the spirit sings,
Embracing all that love can bring.

Through the trials, paths unclear,
We shall walk without the fear.
Trusting in the light we bear,
Finding joy in every prayer.

As we ascend, the world recedes,
Nourished by the sacred deeds.
In our hearts, the truth ignites,
A journey bathed in purest lights.

The Dawn of Understanding

Awake, O heart, to morning's grace,
In every challenge, find your place.
Wisdom whispers in the breeze,
Calling forth the soul to seize.

Each moment, like a sacred gift,
Guides the spirit, gives a lift.
Questions linger, answers near,
In silence, truths become more clear.

The sun ascends with gentle calls,
Illuminating hidden halls.
In every shadow, light conceives,
A path where deeper knowledge weaves.

Harmony in chaos flows,
Teaching hearts what wisdom knows.
In the dawn, we stand renewed,
With understanding's sweet pursuit.

Grateful hearts, in unity,
Bound by love's community.
Together, we shall grow and learn,
In the dawn, the spirit burns.

Transformation in the Stillness

In still waters, spirits cleanse,
Amid the calm, the heart transcends.
Every breath, a chance to grow,
In quietude, the truth we know.

Time slows down, the world recedes,
In the stillness, nature leads.
Transformation starts within,
Where the heart finds peace and kin.

Gentle winds whisper and sigh,
Reminding us of reasons why.
In the power of silence found,
New beginnings, all around.

Let the burdens lift away,
In tranquility, we pray.
For in the hush, the soul takes flight,
Fueled by faith, in sacred light.

From calm waters, ripples spread,
In every heart, a promise bred.
Transformed in stillness, we arise,
With open souls and knowing eyes.

Echoes of the Divine Journey

Through valleys deep, the spirit roams,
Seeking solace, finding homes.
Every footstep, echoes show,
A path where divine rivers flow.

In the heartbeats of the night,
Stars above shine pure and bright.
Guiding travelers onward still,
With grace and love as their goodwill.

As mountains call and rivers bend,
Nature's whispers, soft transcend.
In the journey, truths unfold,
Stories woven, ages old.

With every star, a wish we cast,
In the echoes, shadows past.
Travelers bound by sacred ties,
With faith and dreams, we rise.

In the tapestry of time we weave,
The echoes of our souls believe.
In this journey, joy we glean,
In every whisper, all is seen.

The Holy Awakening

In silence of the night, we pray,
A whisper calls us to the way.
With open hearts, we seek the light,
Divine embrace, our souls take flight.

Awakening in love's embrace,
We find our truth in holy space.
The sacred drum begins to sound,
In unity, our spirits bound.

Eyes opened wide to endless grace,
In every shadow, God's embrace.
We rise together, hand in hand,
On sacred ground, we make our stand.

The dawn of faith, a canvas bright,
Painting hope with strokes of light.
Each heartbeat sings a sacred song,
In every moment, we belong.

Awake, arise, the time is now,
To seek Him deep, to humbly bow.
In holy rapture, we ignite,
The holy awakening of the night.

Balance in the Divine

In the hush of morning's grace,
We find the balance, a sacred place.
Harmony flows in every breath,
A dance of life, beyond of death.

Each moment held in gentle hands,
As heaven whispers, the heart understands.
In light and shadow, truth is found,
The sacred rhythm, a holy sound.

Through trials steep and valleys low,
The path we tread, a sacred flow.
With faith, we walk, united strong,
In balance, we find where we belong.

The stillness deep, the spirit sings,
In every heart, the cosmos brings.
A mirror held to the divine,
We dance in grace, your love, our sign.

In every prayer, a tender touch,
Balancing hearts, we seek so much.
From earth to sky, and back again,
We weave the sacred in every vein.

Journey to the Sacred Garden

A journey calls, the heart takes flight,
To find the garden gloved in light.
Through winding paths and gentle streams,
We walk in faith, we grasp our dreams.

Amidst the blooms, the spirit grows,
In every petal, wisdom flows.
Beneath the boughs, in quiet sighs,
We lift our hearts to endless skies.

Through trial, tears, and whispered prayer,
We find His love is everywhere.
In every stone, in every tree,
The sacred garden sets us free.

With every step, a blessing new,
In every breeze, His promise true.
We seek the path, we hold it dear,
In sacred spaces, He draws near.

The journey ends, but never fades,
In timeless love, our hope cascades.
The sacred garden, forever blooms,
Embraced in grace, where spirit zooms.

The Path of Unseen Blessings

On paths unknown, we wander far,
Guided softly by a star.
In silence deep, the heart can see,
The unseen blessings set us free.

Through shadows cast and trials borne,
The spirit's light in us is sworn.
With every tear and joyful song,
The path reveals where we belong.

With faith in hand, we walk the line,
God's whispers echo, love divine.
A tapestry of grace unfurled,
In prayerful hope, we change the world.

Embrace the journey, trust the way,
For in the night, comes forth the day.
Each challenge faced, a step in grace,
The path of blessings, a holy place.

In gratitude, we find our worth,
A movement of rebirth on earth.
Together we walk, despite the strain,
In unseen blessings, we break the chain.

The Prayer of Our Ascendance

In whispers soft, we raise our hands,
To seek the grace that never ends.
With faith as strong as mountain stone,
We journey forth, never alone.

In stillness find our sacred space,
Where every soul can find its place.
The heavens open, voices blend,
In prayerful hearts, our spirits mend.

Through trials deep, we rise anew,
Each challenge met, each spirit true.
With hope ignited, we ascend,
In unity, our paths extend.

O light divine, our guide and friend,
Together toward the bliss, we wend.
In every heart, Your love's embrace,
We lift our gaze, Your warmth we trace.

Let every moment be a plea,
To live in love, to set us free.
With grateful hearts, we humbly stand,
O Lord, together, hand in hand.

Metamorphosis of the Soul

In shadows deep, the heart does grow,
Through trials faced, the spirit knows.
From ashes rise, like phoenix fire,
Transformation born from pure desire.

In silent hours, the whispers call,
Awakening burdens, heavy thrall.
With every tear, a lesson learned,
Through flickering flames, our souls are turned.

With every dawn, behold the light,
The truth unveiled, now shining bright.
From sorrow's depths, we find our wings,
In freedom's song, the heart now sings.

The chrysalis breaks, the soul takes flight,
In love's embrace, we find our sight.
We shed the past, embrace the now,
With purest grace, we humbly bow.

O lift us high, beyond the veil,
Transform our hearts, let love prevail.
In every beat, a sacred roll,
Rebirth anew, the unbound soul.

Harvesting Lessons of the Divine

In fields of faith, we plant the seeds,
With hope each prayer, our spirit feeds.
The sun may shine, the rains may fall,
In every moment, heed the call.

As seasons change, wisdom unfolds,
In every story, the heart beholds.
We gather strength from trials faced,
In love's embrace, we find our grace.

With open hearts, we tend the soil,
In fellowship, our spirits toil.
The fruits we bear are gifts divine,
In every challenge, a chance to shine.

O learn from nature, gently guide,
In surrender, let love abide.
The lessons learned, forever true,
In unity's dance, we find our view.

From every harvest, blessings pour,
Through gratitude, we seek for more.
In joy we share, the sacred time,
Together woven, heart and rhyme.

The Light Beyond the Horizon

In twilight hues, the sky ignites,
A promise held in coming nights.
Beyond the dark, a beacon glows,
With every breath, the spirit knows.

In whispered winds, the angels sing,
A tale of hope, the dawn will bring.
Illuminated paths unfold,
In courage found, our hearts be bold.

O wanderers, cast fear aside,
In faith's embrace, let love be our guide.
The light beyond, our guiding star,
Connected hearts, though near or far.

With every step, the journey flows,
In sacred moments, our essence grows.
Together, we will chase the light,
With souls united, burning bright.

Beyond the horizon, dreams await,
In sacred trust, we'll navigate.
The dawn will break, bring forth the day,
With love as lantern, come what may.

Rendering the Soul's Maturity

In silence we gather, wisdom's embrace,
A journey within, a sacred place.
The trials we face, refined by the flame,
Each heart a vessel, seeking the same.

With visions of truth, we learn to discern,
In shadows of grief, our spirits can yearn.
The light of the cosmos unveils our deep fears,
Through tears and through joy, we grow through the years.

The echoes of ages resound in our core,
A symphony written in love evermore.
With each passing moment, our essence unfolds,
The path to our wholeness, in stories retold.

In patience, we weave the fabric of grace,
In unity's dance, we find our true place.
Through kindness and mercy, our souls intertwine,
Rendering the essence of love's grand design.

The Sacred Flow of Life

From rivers of grace, the waters do flow,
In whispers of love, the universe glows.
The dance of creation, a rhythm divine,
In each gentle heartbeat, the sacred align.

Beneath the vast heavens, the stars softly gleam,
In every still moment, we enter the dream.
The flowers lift up, their petals in prayer,
In nature's embrace, our burdens laid bare.

With branches that stretch towards the light of the sun,
We gather in circles, each soul a spun one.
The wind carries secrets, the ancient untold,
In the sacred flow, our lives gently unfold.

From mountains to valleys, the echoes resound,
In whispers of truth, our purpose is found.
Embracing the journey, we rise and we fall,
In harmony's essence, we answer the call.

In the Heart of Transformation

In the chrysalis state, we shed our old skin,
Awakening dreams where new lives begin.
With courage ignited, we venture to see,
The beauty of change as we blossom to be.

In darkness, we wander, yet stars guide our way,
The trials of night usher in a new day.
With whispers of wisdom, the universe sings,
In the heart of our struggle, true freedom springs.

With ashes and echoes, rebirth will arise,
In faith we transform, revealing our skies.
As rivers converge, our spirits align,
In the heart of this journey, our destinies twine.

Through valleys of sorrow, we sow seeds of grace,
In the tapestry woven, we find our own place.
With love as our compass, our souls take to flight,
In the heart of transformation, we shine ever bright.

The Rising of Eternal Souls

In the dawn of creation, the light softly breaks,
A promise of love in the stillness awakes.
With eyes full of wonder, we gaze at the morn,
Awakening spirits, in hope we are born.

Through struggles and shadows, we find our own way,
With faith as our beacon, we rise to the day.
The strength of our hearts, an unyielding force,
In the rising of souls, we honor the course.

With laughter and tears, we dance 'neath the skies,
In bonds of connection, our spirits arise.
From valleys of sorrow, and mountains of glee,
The essence of peace flows eternally free.

In circles we gather, united as one,
Underneath the vast heavens, a journey begun.
With voices resounding, a heavenly call,
In the rising of souls, we discover our all.

The Faithful Journey of Becoming

In every heart, a whisper sings,
A calling deep as spirit springs,
With every step, we find our way,
In faith we trust, through night and day.

Each stumble teaches us to rise,
With open soul, we seek the skies,
Through trials faced, our strength we gain,
In sacred love, we shall remain.

The road is long, yet never bare,
With loyal hearts, we heed the prayer,
Each moment, grace within us flows,
As truth within our being grows.

Let kindness be our guiding light,
In every shadow, spark the bright,
With open hands, we share our bread,
In every tear, a tale is read.

The journey binds us, one and all,
In perfect love, we rise, we fall,
A tapestry of souls entwined,
In faith, a deeper path we find.

In the Shadow of Loss, We Blossom

In silence wrapped, the heart does weep,
Yet seeds of hope, beneath pain's steep,
From depths of sorrow, strength will rise,
In loss, we find our truest ties.

Each tear a river, flowing free,
A testament of love's decree,
Through shadows cast, light will emerge,
In grief, we hold the sacred urge.

Remembered smiles in whispered prayer,
A legacy that lingers there,
From ashes gray, new blooms will spring,
In every heart, a song to sing.

The cycle turns, the seasons shift,
In loss, the spirit learns to lift,
With every breath, the past embraced,
In love's pure light, we're interlaced.

So let us walk, though shadows loom,
In every heart, a sacred room,
Where memory shines, and love prevails,
In loss, we join the winding trails.

The Light of Understanding

In every thought, a spark ignites,
A quest for truth, through day and nights,
In stillness found, the soul takes flight,
With open eyes, we seek the light.

Through winding paths, the questions roam,
In every heart, the quest for home,
With gentle hands, we share our fears,
In wisdom's light, we'll dry our tears.

The lessons learned, in warmth and care,
In every heart, a flame we share,
With patience guides, through dark and bright,
In understanding, we find our sight.

Let love be loud, in hearts and hands,
In harmony, our spirit stands,
Together strong, we rise anew,
In every challenge, grace breaks through.

So walk with me, in faith we'll stand,
With hearts united, hand in hand,
For in this journey, truth we find,
In light of love, we're intertwined.

The Holy Cycle of Growth

In nature's arms, the seed is sown,
With tender care, the garden grown,
From earth to sky, our spirits lift,
In every moment, life's sweet gift.

Through seasons' dance, we change and grow,
With every breath, the rivers flow,
In sunlit days and moonlit nights,
Our souls evolve, in sacred rites.

Embrace the rain, let shadows fall,
In every try, rise from the stall,
For in each challenge, strength is found,
In holy cycles, love abound.

Let kindness be the roots we share,
With open hearts, we learn to care,
In giving, receiving, we unite,
With faith and hope, our spirits bright.

So join the dance, let life's song ring,
In every note, our spirits sing,
For in this cycle, grace reflects,
The holy growth that life protects.

The Altar of Our Evolution

Upon the altar, we gather near,
The whispers of ages, we hold dear.
Evolution calls with a sacred tune,
Guiding our hearts to the light of noon.

Each step we take on this hallowed ground,
In grace and humility, our souls are found.
Time flows like water, a river of truth,
Nurturing wisdom, eternal in youth.

The stones beneath speak of trials faced,
In unity's name, we're lovingly graced.
Together we rise, transcend and behold,
The mysteries written in love untold.

With every breath, the divine we seek,
In silence we listen, in prayer we speak.
For the altar stands firm, unwavering in light,
A testament found in the depths of night.

In the heart of our journey, we find our way,
Through shadows and doubts, we choose to stay.
The altar of evolution, a sacred design,
Where spirit and matter eternally align.

The Path of Sacred Understanding

On the path of light, we walk so bold,
Each lesson unfolds like a story told.
In stillness we gather, in wonder we learn,
Seeking the truths for which our hearts yearn.

With every step, we hold compassion,
A warm embrace in divine fashion.
The stars above guide us, bright as the sun,
In unity's spirit, we all are one.

Through trials that shape our very core,
We rise in faith, we break down the door.
The whispers of wisdom, a gentle nudge,
Leading us forward, we will not judge.

As rivers flow deep into the sea,
So too do our hearts crave unity.
With open minds, we delve into grace,
Transforming our spirits, we find our place.

Together we weave a tapestry bright,
Of sacred understanding, shining with light.
With peace as our guide, our burdens will wane,
On the path of love, we shall remain.

Blossoms of the Spirit

In gardens of faith, the spirit blooms,
With petals of hope, dispelling the glooms.
Each blossom a prayer, each fragrance a song,
Whispers of love in the heart, so strong.

The seeds of compassion, in silence, we sow,
Nurtured in kindness, they blossom and grow.
Together we flourish, in harmony's dance,
In the light of the sacred, we take our chance.

The colors unite in a radiant flow,
Painting our world with a vibrant glow.
In moments of trial, when shadows conspire,
The blossoms remind us of love's sweet fire.

As blooms greet the dawn with their joyful cheer,
They beckon the weary to come and draw near.
In the garden of souls, we each play a part,
Tending the blossoms that bloom in the heart.

So let us embrace each flower we find,
The beauty of spirit, in love intertwined.
For in every blossom, the divine we see,
A reminder that together, we all can be free.

From the Cradle to Eternity

From the cradle's warmth to the skies above,
A journey as sacred as the stars that move.
With each tiny heartbeat, a promise unfolds,
A tale of existence in whispers retold.

In the arms of creation, we learn and we grow,
With every heartbeat, love's river will flow.
Through laughter and tears, we lie side by side,
In the cradle of grace, where spirits abide.

As seasons will turn and the years will glide,
We gather the moments, our hearts open wide.
With the wisdom of ages, we cherish the past,
Knowing the light of eternity will last.

With faith as our compass, we navigate time,
Each challenge embraced, through mountains we climb.
From the first breath drawn to the last, we'll see,
The cradle of love will forever be free.

So let us journey from now until then,
In the embrace of the sacred, once again.
For from the cradle, we rise without fear,
To eternity's arms, forever held near.

Notes from the Sacred Journey

In silence we tread on a path so bright,
With faith as our guide, we embrace the light.
Each step we take, a prayer in the night,
The spirit awakens, taking its flight.

Mountains arise, with wisdom to share,
The valleys below, filled with love and care.
We carry our burdens, our hearts laid bare,
Each moment a gift, a treasure so rare.

Through storms we march, with courage ablaze,
In every struggle, we seek to give praise.
For in our trials, the soul learns to gaze,
Upon the divine in the simplest ways.

We gather like leaves in the autumn's embrace,
In unity formed, we find sacred space.
Through whispers of peace, we're touched by grace,
Together we walk, in love we efface.

At journey's end, with hearts intertwined,
We'll find the true essence of love, unconfined.
In realms of existence, forever aligned,
In notes of the sacred, our spirits refined.

The Covenant of Blossoms

In the garden of faith, blossoms unfold,
Each petal a story, in colors so bold.
We nurture the roots, where love can take hold,
In the covenant made, let our hearts be told.

Fragrant whispers arise through the air,
In prayers of gratitude, we learn to share.
The beauty of life, in each moment, we care,
Together in spirit, no burden we bear.

As seasons do change, the blossoms renew,
With lessons of patience in every hue.
In planting our seeds, we find strength in the few,
The promise of growth in the morning dew.

Through trials and storms, we rise to each call,
In unity fierce, we will never fall.
With arms open wide, we embrace one and all,
Cultivating hope in the shades of the fall.

When petals drift down, like prayers in the breeze,
We honor the past and the memories seize.
In love's gentle touch, our spirits find ease,
In the covenant of blossoms, our hearts are at peace.

Seasons of the Spirit

In the spring of our souls, new life will emerge,
With blossoms of labor in love's gentle surge.
Each heartbeat a promise, each moment a urge,
Awakening spirits, in grace we converge.

Summer sun shines, casting warmth to our days,
In the light we gather, with joyful displays.
Through laughter and music, the heart gently sways,
United in harmony, we find our ways.

Autumn arrives, with reflections in gold,
The harvest of wisdom, the stories retold.
In gratitude whispered, our spirits behold,
The beauty of change, as life does unfold.

Winter's embrace, with its solemn retreat,
In silence and stillness, our hearts feel the beat.
The flame of devotion guides us to meet,
The essence of spirit, in darkness we greet.

Each season a chapter, a lesson divine,
Through valleys and peaks, in faith we align.
In every transition, the soul will refine,
Through seasons of spirit, our hearts intertwine.

The Alchemy of Divine Lessons

In the crucible of life, we forge our way,
Through trials and blessings, we learn to pray.
Each moment a lesson, each choice a display,
Transforming the heart in a sacred ballet.

With faith as our compass, we navigate choice,
In whispers of wisdom, we hear the still voice.
Through shadows of doubt, we rise and rejoice,
In every reflection, let love be the noise.

The alchemist's touch flows through each belief,
In the furnace of hope, we create our relief.
From pain to the grace, we find sweet reprieve,
In the tapestry woven, we learn to achieve.

With open hands raised, we offer our trust,
In surrender we blossom, a promise we must.
Through cycles of giving, from stardust to dust,
In the alchemy of life, our spirits combust.

Hand in hand moving, through light and through dark,
Each lesson a flame, igniting the spark.
In the dance of existence, our spirits embark,
Transforming our souls, we leave a bright mark.

Echoes of Faithful Transformation

In whispers soft, the spirit calls,
Awakening hope where darkness falls.
In trials faced, our hearts unite,
Transforming shadows into light.

With gentle hands, the Creator molds,
A tapestry of faith unfolds.
Through tears of joy and pain we find,
The sacred path by love defined.

Each step we take, a vow to keep,
In silent prayers from hearts so deep.
We rise like dawn, from ashes soar,
Embracing grace forevermore.

The mirror shows a heart renewed,
In every trial, a chance to brood.
Echoes of faith, we carry near,
Guiding us through, beyond all fear.

In quiet moments, truth will gleam,
A light that fuels a shared dream.
The journey bends but never breaks,
For love abides, and grace awakes.

The Pilgrimage of the Heart

Upon this road, our souls embark,
With every step, we seek the spark.
In distant lands, both near and far,
We find our compass in the star.

The burdens borne, we lay them down,
Each step a jewel, each laugh a crown.
Through valleys low and mountains high,
In faith, we learn to spread our wings and fly.

Whispers linger in the breeze,
Soft guidance found beneath the trees.
With open hearts, we share our love,
A journey blessed from God above.

For every road that twists and turns,
A flame within, our spirit burns.
We gather strength from those we meet,
Our paths entwined, a sacred feat.

The night may fall, but dawn will rise,
With every trial, wisdom lies.
The pilgrimage, our hearts refine,
In every moment, His love we find.

The Sacred Transition

In sacred time, the world will shift,
Awakening hearts, the greatest gift.
When layers peel, and truth is shown,
A seed of faith, in spirit sown.

With every breath, a promise made,
In silent vows, we are remade.
The ebb and flow, the dance of grace,
In every shadow, we find His face.

The hourglass spills its golden sand,
We grasp the threads, entwined by hand.
Through every trial, we emerge bright,
In sacred transitions, we find our light.

From dusk to dawn, our spirits rise,
With open hearts and grateful sighs.
The journey guides, the river flows,
In every moment, His love bestows.

The stillness speaks, we hear the call,
In every heart, His whispers fall.
A sacred transition, we embrace,
In trust and joy, we find our place.

Unfolding in the Grace of Time

In quiet hours, His love reveals,
Through tangled paths, our spirit heals.
With every breath, the promise grows,
In gentle winds, His presence flows.

As seasons pass, we're transformed anew,
In every heartbeat, grace shines through.
With open hands, we learn to share,
The beauty found in love and care.

For every tear that graces skin,
A miracle stirs, awakening within.
In gratitude we rise and sing,
Unfolding joys that each day brings.

The path may twist, the light may wane,
Yet in His arms, we feel no pain.
In the dance of life, a rhythm divine,
We move in step, unfolding in time.

With hearts aligned, we seek the way,
In every dawn and fading day.
The grace of time, a sacred seam,
In every moment, we weave our dream.

Embracing the Divine Seasons

In spring's embrace, blooms arise,
Awakening hearts under brightening skies.
Each petal whispers, a sacred call,
Nature's tune sings, inviting us all.

Summer's warmth, a radiant light,
Guiding our steps through day and night.
In the dance of sun, shadows play,
We find our truth amid the fray.

Autumn's grace, leaves gently fall,
A tapestry woven, each hue a thrall.
In rustling whispers, lessons unfold,
The wisdom of ages, silently told.

Winter's quiet, a time for rest,
In frozen stillness, our spirits are blessed.
Yearning for warmth, yet finding peace,
In the heart of cold, our souls release.

Through each season, the Divine we seek,
Embracing the journey, humble and meek.
With open hearts, we learn to believe,
In nature's chorus, we join and weave.

The Wings of Faithful Transformation

In the cocoon, darkness lies,
A promise kept beneath the skies.
Faith unfurls with gentle grace,
Emerging beauty begins to trace.

The chrysalis breaks, wings take flight,
A dance of colors, pure delight.
From shadows deep to skies so wide,
In every struggle, love will guide.

With each new dawn, hope reinvents,
The spirit soars, the heart laments.
Yet through the trials, we are refined,
In sacred growth, purpose aligned.

The winds of change, a divine breath,
In every ending, a promise kept.
Transformation, the song we sing,
In the act of faith, new life takes wing.

So let us rise and leave behind,
Old burdens shed, new paths defined.
In faithful flight, together we soar,
Through skies of promise, forevermore.

The Symphony of Quiet Faith

In silent prayers, the heart takes flight,
With whispered hopes amid the night.
Each thought a note in a sacred hymn,
A melody soft, where shadows dim.

The gentle breeze carries our plea,
In the stillness, divine harmony.
Each breath we take, a sacred pause,
In quiet trust, we find our cause.

The stars above, a guiding light,
In the darkness, they shine so bright.
With every moment, faith's embrace,
A symphony found in time and space.

Our souls entwined in a tender throng,
In the echo of faith, we belong.
Through life's cadence, we hear the call,
In the silence, we rise, we fall.

Let our hearts beat in sacred tune,
With each new day, under the moon.
A symphony woven by grace divine,
In the hush of faith, our spirits align.

The Tides of Celestial Maturity

In the ebb and flow, wisdom grows,
Each wave a lesson, as nature shows.
Tides of grace, pull and release,
In surrender, we find our peace.

As moons align, the heart expands,
With every phase, we learn to stand.
In the depths of change, courage swells,
Navigating life, where the soul dwells.

With every storm, we gain a sight,
The beauty found in the darkest night.
Through trials faced, our spirits mend,
In the river of time, on love we depend.

As seasons shift and cycles turn,
In the heart of chaos, wisdom we earn.
Maturity blooms in sacred tides,
In the journey we're on, the Divine abides.

So let us flow with the cosmic song,
Trusting the tides, where we belong.
In surrender and grace, we find our way,
Through the celestial dance of night and day.

Ascending Through the Years

With every dawn, our spirits rise,
Guided by faith, we touch the skies.
Moments of grace, in whispers found,
In the heart's silence, love knows no bound.

Each step we take, a sacred thread,
We weave our path, where angels tread.
Through trials faced, our souls ignite,
In the dance of shadows, we find the light.

Time flows onward, a river's grace,
Carrying dreams to a holy place.
In every sorrow, joy intertwines,
For in our struggles, His love defines.

As the seasons turn, we shall behold,
The stories of faith that have been told.
With open hearts, we rise anew,
In each embracing, He walks with you.

So let us climb, hand in hand,
Up the mountain, where truth does stand.
Through every year, we come alive,
In the warmth of love, we shall thrive.

The Divine Tapestry of Time

On the loom of fate, we weave our way,
Threads of hope in colors play.
Every moment, a strand of grace,
In the sacred weave, we find our place.

The hands of time, both gentle and bold,
Mend our hearts, both young and old.
In the fabric rich, our stories blend,
Bound by the love that knows no end.

Every heartbeat, a note in the song,
Echoing praises, where we belong.
Through the trials, the fears, the pain,
Our faith remains, like summer rain.

In stillness found, the spirit glows,
Guiding us through as each season flows.
Together we stand, in joy, in strife,
For in the tapestry, we find our life.

So let us cherish the fibers tight,
In the tapestry woven with purest light.
For every thread, a tale unfolds,
In the hands of the Divine, our hearts consoled.

Seeds of Tomorrow's Light

In the soil of faith, we plant our dreams,
Nurtured with love, they sprout like beams.
With every prayer, a flower blooms,
In the garden of hope, dispelling glooms.

Through seasons' change, our roots grow deep,
In fertile ground, our promise we keep.
Each seed a wish, each bud a prayer,
For tomorrow's dawn, our hearts laid bare.

The sun bestows its grace divine,
While rain of mercy, like blessings, shine.
With patience held, we cultivate,
The light of promise, we celebrate.

In the embrace of the growing light,
We chase the shadows, dispelling night.
With every harvest, our spirits sing,
For in these seeds, eternity springs.

So let us sow with joy and care,
Trusting in love, our souls laid bare.
For in our hearts, the seeds take flight,
Transforming darkness into radiant light.

Journeys in Sacred Growth

In paths unknown, we start our quest,
With faith as guide, we find our rest.
Through valleys low and mountains high,
In every struggle, we learn to fly.

The teacher within whispers so soft,
In trials faced, our spirits loft.
Each step forward, a lesson learned,
In every corner, the heart discerned.

With open eyes, we see the signs,
In sacred moments, His love aligns.
Every detour leads us near,
To the truth that banishes fear.

With hands extended, we lift the weak,
In the embrace of love, we speak.
For in our journeys, together we grow,
In the bond of faith, our light will glow.

So let us wander the winding way,
In sacred growth, we choose to stay.
For through each trial, together we burn,
In the heart of the journey, our souls return.

Strength in the Quietude

In the stillness, hearts align,
Faith is whispered, soft divine.
Hope like rivers, gently flows,
In quietude, our spirit grows.

When the world is loud and bold,
Silence speaks, a truth untold.
In the hush, we find our might,
Guided by the inner light.

Moments linger, time stands still,
In the calm, we find our will.
Through the shadows, we shall tread,
With quiet strength, we're gently led.

Each heartbeat sings a sacred song,
In solitude, we all belong.
Embrace the still, the gentle hand,
Together here, we firmly stand.

The journey slow, yet ever true,
In quietude, His love anew.
We hold the faith, a simple creed,
In silence found, our souls are freed.

Whispered Prayers of Change

With every breath, a prayer we weave,
In whispered tones, we do believe.
From deep within, our voices rise,
To touch the heavens, pierce the skies.

Change comes softly through the night,
In shadowed corners, seeking light.
God hears the sighs, the dreams we share,
In the quiet, answers flare.

Each moment framed in love and grace,
Whispered prayers, a sacred space.
Transform the heart, renew the mind,
In gentle strength, our souls rewind.

Through trials faced and storms we weather,
We find our peace when hearts are tethered.
In the silence, bold voices sing,
Of hope and love and every thing.

Every heartbeat holds a tale,
In prayers whispered, we prevail.
Together we rise, we strive to change,
In faith and trust, our lives rearrange.

Altar of Dreams

On the altar, dreams are laid,
With whispered hopes, our fears displayed.
In sacred trust, we place our pain,
For love will heal, and hope remain.

Each aspiration, bright and clear,
Brought to Him with love sincere.
In the stillness, visions grow,
Guided by the light we sow.

The past is gone, the future's bright,
In faith and prayer, we find our light.
With every tear, a seed is sown,
In the garden of our own.

Together we dream, together we rise,
In the glow of the evening skies.
Embracing whispers, love's sweet grace,
In the altar of dreams, we find our place.

With open hearts, we seek and learn,
In every dream, we take our turn.
For in our hopes, divinely crafted,
Faithful souls are ever uplifted.

From Shadows to Radiance

In shadows deep, the spirit waits,
For light to guide through heavy gates.
Each step we take, a path unfurls,
As dawn approaches, darkness swirls.

From night's embrace, we draw the grace,
In every struggle, find our place.
With faith as armor, hearts ignite,
Transforming pain into the light.

The journey long, through valleys cold,
In whispered prayers, our strength is bold.
We rise anew, in love's embrace,
From shadows lost to radiance.

Each moment shines, a precious gift,
As hope arises, spirits lift.
Together we flourish, hand in hand,
In light's warm glow, together stand.

Every dawn is a promise bright,
A pathway forged from dark to light.
With every heartbeat, grace we find,
From shadows lost, our souls entwined.

In Divine Abundance We Flourish

In the bounty of grace, we find our way,
Each dawn a blessing, a brand new day.
With hearts united in faith we stand,
Together we tread on this sacred land.

In joy we gather, in love's embrace,
We share the light, the warmth of His grace.
Grateful whispers rise, like fragrant prayer,
In divine abundance, none shall despair.

Through trials fierce, our spirits grow,
With every challenge, the faith we sow.
From seeds of hope, great trees arise,
In heavenly gardens where love never dies.

With every heartbeat, His promise rings,
In the dance of life, our souls take wings.
We flourish together, in unity we bloom,
In the light of His love, we dispel the gloom.

In peace we gather, our voices blend,
In the sacred circle, where all hearts mend.
Together we rise, hand in hand with grace,
In divine abundance, we find our place.

The Spirited Ascend

In the morning light, the spirit awakes,
With every breath, the heart gently breaks.
A yearning to rise, to touch the divine,
In the vast expanse, His glory we find.

Through trials we climb, with faith as our guide,
Each step is a prayer, with angels beside.
In love's great embrace, we soar ever high,
The spirit ascends, like a bird in the sky.

In silence we listen, to whispers so sweet,
The call of the heavens beneath our feet.
With courage ignited, our passions ignite,
In the arms of the Lord, we will take flight.

Through valleys and peaks, our journey unfolds,
With stories of grace, and wisdom untold.
In unity striving, we rise up anew,
Through the Spirit's embrace, we're born from the blue.

With eyes set on stars, our mission ignites,
In devotion we gather, igniting the nights.
For the spirited ascend, to realms ever bright,
In the dance of creation, we embrace the light.

The Serenity of Inner Bloom

In the quiet stillness, the soul finds peace,
From the depths of chaos, a sweet release.
With each gentle breath, the heart blossoms wide,
In the sanctuary of silence, where love does abide.

Amidst the chaos, a garden does grow,
In whispers of hope, great blessings overflow.
Petals of patience unfurl in the sun,
In the serenity of spirit, we are all one.

Through trials and tests, we nurture the seed,
With faith as our water, and love's gentle need.
In the stillness we find, the beauty within,
In the grace of forgiveness, our journey begins.

In moments of doubt, the light gently breaks,
With courage and kindness, the heart overtakes.
Each moment's a gift, a chance to renew,
In the serenity of inner bloom, we pursue.

So let us tend lovingly, this garden of grace,
In unity rising, together we face.
As petals unfold, in the warmth of His love,
In the serenity of inner bloom, we rise above.

God's Garden of Transformations

In the garden of faith, our spirits entwine,
Where seeds of compassion, in love's soil combine.
Each transformation, a dance of the heart,
In God's gentle hands, we become a new part.

Amongst vibrant colors, our spirits take flight,
In the warmth of His love, we bask in the light.
With joy in our hearts and hope in our eyes,
In God's garden of grace, our spirits arise.

Through shadows and storms, we learn to grow strong,
In the embrace of the Lord, where we all belong.
With faith as our compass, through trials we stride,
In God's wondrous garden, forever our guide.

In moments of stillness, His presence we see,
In the beauty of nature, we set our hearts free.
For each flower that blooms tells a story divine,
In God's garden of transformations, love will shine.

Let every heart open, to the blessings that flow,
In the richness of grace, we find our glow.
With gratitude flowing, we dance in His light,
In God's garden of transformations, all is bright.

Transcending the Ordinary

In quiet depths, a whisper stirs,
The heart's soft hymn to the divine.
Beyond the veil, a light occurs,
In stillness found, we intertwine.

Each moment glows, a sacred chance,
To rise above the mundane line.
With faith, we step, we start to dance,
As grace reveals what love can find.

The daily grind, a fleeting dream,
Yet in our souls, the truth will bloom.
We glimpse the world as pure and clean,
Where love transcends, dispelling gloom.

Awake and aware, we seek the path,
Where doubt dissolves in faith's embrace.
With open hearts, we feel the wrath,
Of overcoming every trace.

So let us soar in spirit's flight,
Beyond the shadows, into light.
Our journey's blessed with grace so bright,
Transcending all, we find our sight.

Climbing the Mountain of Belief

With each step firm, the path ascends,
Through trials steep, our spirits rise.
The summit calls, where love transcends,
To see the world through sacred eyes.

The air grows thin, yet hope abounds,
Each heartbeat echoes faith's pure song.
In every struggle, strength resounds,
We journey forth, where we belong.

The rocks may shift, the winds may howl,
But anchored deep in truth we stand.
With courage firm, we heed the vow,
To reach the heights, we join our hands.

In prayerful breaths, we find our grace,
The mountain lifts us ever high.
In unity, we seek the place,
Where faith and love can never die.

At last we stand, the view unfolds,
The valley vast, our spirits soar.
The story written, pure and bold,
In climbing here, we've found much more.

A Covenant of Growth

In sacred soil, our roots entwine,
Each promise made, a tender shoot.
With time and care, the hearts align,
To blossom forth, our faith takes root.

With gentle hands, we nurture prayer,
As light breaks forth, the shadows flee.
In love's embrace, we grow to share,
A constant dance, forever free.

Through seasons change, we stand our ground,
With unity, we weather storms.
In every challenge, hope is found,
Together formed, our spirits warm.

As branches stretch, our vision grows,
To touch the skies, our dreams take flight.
In every heart, a river flows,
In faith, we find our guiding light.

A covenant true, we'll stand as one,
In freedom's grace, our spirits blend.
With every day, new life begun,
In joy and love, our souls ascend.

Boundless Horizons of the Spirit

In realms where faith and hope reside,
We journey forth, our spirits free.
Beyond the dusk, the dawn will guide,
To places where our hearts can see.

Each gentle breeze, a whisper clear,
In every step, a song of grace.
The love we share, a bond sincere,
To lift us high in this vast space.

With eyes unclouded, we seek the truth,
In stars above, in hearts aglow.
We find the wisdom of the youth,
In memories shared, our spirits grow.

No bounds can hold the soul's pure flight,
We rise like eagles, wings outspread.
In every trial, we find the light,
With courage strong, we're gently led.

So let us soar on winds of joy,
With grateful hearts, we'll make our mark.
In loving bonds, we can't destroy,
Boundless horizons, our spirits spark.

Sacred Steps of the Soul

In silence we walk, with faith as our guide,
Each footstep a whisper, where love does abide.
The heart beats in rhythm, a song divine,
With each sacred moment, the soul intertwines.

Through valleys of shadow, the light starts to gleam,
With courage our vessel, we sail on a dream.
A prayer softly spoken, a bond that is true,
The grace of existence shines brightly anew.

On mountains of mercy, we gather our hope,
With hands joined in purpose, together we cope.
Each challenge a lesson, each sorrow a chance,
To nourish our spirits, in love's sweet expanse.

With wisdom of ages, and hearts full of fire,
We rise like the morning, renewed and inspired.
In the dance of devotion, we find our own way,
The sacred steps guide us, through night and through day.

As dawn paints the sky with a tender embrace,
We stand hand in hand, in this holy place.
For every soul wandering, there's peace to be won,
In sacred steps taken, we shine like the sun.

Harvesting the Light Within

In the garden of spirit, where dreams start to grow,
We gather the moments, and let the love flow.
With each breath a blessing, so tender and bright,
We're harvesting wisdom, in the stillness of night.

With faith as our compass, we nurture the seeds,
Of hope and compassion, fulfilling our needs.
In the rhythm of life, every heartbeat we share,
Transforms into petals that fragrance the air.

As the sun goes down, we embrace the unknown,
In the depths of our hearts, a bright light has shone.
Through trials we gather, the courage to stand,
In the richness of love, we find common land.

With hands open wide, we receive and we give,
In the cycle of kindness, we flourish and live.
The harvest we carry, for all to partake,
Is a banquet of blessings, for love's sacred sake.

And in stillness we kneel, in gratitude's grace,
For the light we have nurtured, in this hallowed space.
Together we flourish, in union we thrive,
Harvesting light, our souls come alive.

Illuminated Hearts

In the glow of the evening, we gather in peace,
With hearts intertwined, our worries release.
Each spirit a beacon, shining so bright,
Illuminated souls, we embrace the divine light.

Through shadows of doubt, our faith becomes clear,
With whispers of angels, we draw ever near.
In the warmth of connection, we feel love's embrace,
Every moment a treasure, a sacred trace.

United we sing, in the stillness of night,
With voices like echoes, we soar to new heights.
In the tapestry woven by grace and by chance,
We dance in the light, as we join in the trance.

With gratitude flowing, our spirits ignite,
In the canvas of life, each heart becomes bright.
Together we journey, in faith we abide,
Illuminated hearts, in love we confide.

So let us be flames, that flicker and burn,
With hope as our guide, for love we shall yearn.
In this beautiful union, our souls take flight,
Illuminated by grace, we'll shine through the night.

The Evolution of Grace

In the flow of existence, where time starts to bend,
We witness the changes, as spirits ascend.
With each breath a lesson, a moment to find,
The evolution of grace, is the dance of the mind.

Through valleys of sorrow, where shadows reside,
We learn from the darkness, with love as our guide.
With open hearts tender, we rise from our fall,
In the journey of grace, we answer the call.

With every step taken, the journey unfolds,
In stories of wisdom, our truth is retold.
For every heart wounded, there's strength that remains,
In the evolution of grace, we break all the chains.

As rivers of kindness flow deep in our veins,
We breathe in the love, that forever sustains.
With courage and patience, we light up our way,
In the evolution of grace, we choose to stay.

Together we blossom, in unity's fire,
For the path of grace leads us ever higher.
With souls intertwined, we embrace the unknown,
In the evolution of grace, we're never alone.

Seeds of Everlasting Peace

In the quiet hush of dawn,
We plant our dreams in sacred soil.
Each seed a prayer for love to spawn,
Watered by faith and gentle toil.

With every sprout a message clear,
The bonds of mercy intertwine.
In hearts once gripped by doubt and fear,
Now bloom the flowers of divine.

As sunlight warms the tender fold,
We gather hope in hand and heart.
The stories of the faithful told,
In unity, we play our part.

So let us rise through trials faced,
With kindness as our guiding star.
In acts of love, forever graced,
We find our home, no matter how far.

Together, in this garden vast,
We sow the seeds, embrace the peace.
In harmony, our shadows cast,
A legacy that shall not cease.

The Radiant Ascent

Upon the hill, where shadows fade,
We climb the path towards the light.
With lighter hearts, our fears unmade,
Each step reveals the day so bright.

Awake, O soul, to truth sublime,
For in the stillness, know we rise.
In every whisper, every chime,
The radiance flows from whispered skies.

The angels tread this sacred way,
They guide our hearts through misty morn.
With every breath, we start to sway,
To melodies of love reborn.

Fear not the heights, embrace the climb,
For every journey leads us home.
With faith, we find the pulse of time,
In unity, no need to roam.

Not lost in darkness, we find grace,
In every challenge, every bend.
The radiant ascent, our rightful place,
Where love and hope shall never end.

Attuning to the Divine

In silence, hearts begin to mend,
Amidst the noise, we find our song.
Each moment spent, our souls transcend,
Attuning to the sacred throng.

With every prayer, a note we send,
To realms of peace beyond our sight.
As echoes of creation blend,
We dance with joy, embraced by light.

The stillness speaks, a gentle guide,
In shadows cast, our truth we find.
Together, we walk side by side,
With open hearts and open minds.

Each breath a step toward the Divine,
In nature's hymn, we hear the call.
With love and grace, our spirits align,
A symphony that lifts us all.

So let us gather in this space,
And feel the pulse of love divine.
In unity, we find our grace,
Attuning to the light we shine.

The Graces of Time

In fleeting hours, wisdom flows,
Each moment's touch, a sacred gift.
Through seasons past, our spirit grows,
In every trial, we learn to lift.

The morning dawns with gentle grace,
Awakens dreams from slumber deep.
In time's embrace, we find our place,
As memories in our hearts we keep.

With every heartbeat, life's refrain,
A melody of joy and pain.
In love's sweet dance, we break the chain,
Transforming sorrow into gain.

So cherish now, the present's light,
For every joy is born in time.
With gratitude, we take flight,
Embracing each moment so sublime.

As years unfold, we weave our tale,
A tapestry of grace and love.
In every breath, let hearts prevail,
For we are blessed by grace above.

The Miracle of Renewal

In morning's light, our spirits rise,
Awakening grace from the skies.
With hope reborn in every heart,
A sacred journey, a brand new start.

Through trials faced and shadows cast,
We find our strength, our faith held fast.
Each drop of rain, a tear that's shed,
Gives life anew where once was dread.

From barren soil, the flowers bloom,
A testament to dispel all gloom.
In every breath, the promise flows,
A miracle that gently grows.

With open arms, we welcome change,
Transforming self, we will arrange.
In solitude we seek His face,
In every moment, find His grace.

And as the seasons turn and spin,
We shed the past, the light within.
A cycle vast, yet tender too,
Forever bound, the old and new.

Rebirth in Reverence

As dawn awakens, whispers sweet,
The world rejoices, dreams repeat.
In solemn prayer, our hearts take flight,
Embracing hope with pure delight.

Each soul reflects a sacred tale,
In every grief, our spirits sail.
Beneath the stars, we cast our fears,
In faith's embrace, we shed our tears.

The shadows fade with every call,
In love's embrace, we rise, not fall.
A gentle touch, a hand of grace,
In silent reverence, we find our place.

Our paths converge in quiet bliss,
In moments shared, we seek His kiss.
As flowers bloom in twilight's glow,
We honor life, the seeds we sow.

With every heartbeat, renewed we stand,
In sacred circles, hand in hand.
The journey long, yet blessed we find,
Rebirth awaits, in truth aligned.

The Mosaic of Our Paths

In unity, we weave our ways,
Painting life in vibrant rays.
Each step adorned with colors bright,
A tapestry of faith and light.

The past and present, intertwined,
In the hands of grace, divinely designed.
With every experience, wisdom shared,
A mosaic crafted, love declared.

Through trials faced and mountains climbed,
The threads of strength in hearts combined.
With laughter, tears, a mixed embrace,
In every moment, we find our place.

As life's design unfolds with time,
We dance to rhythms, a sacred rhyme.
In fellowship, our spirits soar,
A masterpiece, forevermore.

With every heartbeat, we create,
A mosaic that reflects our fate.
Together strong, we rise and stand,
In divine love, hand in hand.

Radiance Beyond the Veil

In silence deep, the truth awaits,
Beyond the veil, the spirit mates.
With every breath, we glimpse the light,
A radiance divine, forever bright.

The whispers soft, the heart's decree,
In shadows cast, we long to see.
With every prayer, a sacred plea,
To touch the realm of eternity.

Through trials faced, we search for peace,
In love's embrace, our fears release.
The journey long, yet souls are bold,
In radiance, our stories told.

As stars align, the time draws near,
With open hearts, cast away fear.
Together bound by sacred trust,
In every moment, rise we must.

Beyond the veil, the light we find,
A spark divine within mankind.
With faith, we soar on wings of grace,
Eternal love, our saving place.

Lessons Carved in Faith

In the stillness of the night,
Whispers of wisdom call my name.
Foundations built on love's pure light,
Hearts ignited, never the same.

Through trials that sculpt the soul,
Each moment a lesson shared.
In faith we rise, we become whole,
A journey divinely prepared.

Hands that tremble, prayers take flight,
Chasing shadows, finding grace.
In the battles, we find our might,
Hope reflected in every face.

With every doubt, a seed is sown,
In gardens where spirits soar.
Belief, the quiet undertone,
Unites us forevermore.

So let us stand through fire and rain,
In the truth that leads us home.
For every joy, there's wisdom's gain,
In faith, together, we roam.

The Everlasting Embrace of Change

In the river of time we flow,
Every moment, a sacred gift.
Embracing the tides, we learn to grow,
As shadows and light begin to shift.

Season's whispers dance in the air,
Nature's palette painted bright.
Change, a canvas for hearts laid bare,
In stillness, we find our sight.

Leaves may fall, yet roots run deep,
Life cycles weave a grand design.
In surrender, the spirit leaps,
Found in the fabric of the divine.

With every dawn, let go of yesterday,
Unfold what was written in the stars.
For in the journey, we find our way,
Healing the world, mending the scars.

So let us dance in this sacred flow,
Trusting the path beneath our feet.
In the embrace of change, we glow,
For every end births something sweet.

The Quiet Kilns of Growth

In the hearth of the heart, a fire burns,
Soft embers whisper tales untold.
From ashes arise the lessons learned,
In patience, the spirit unfolds.

Through trials, the clay is shaped anew,
Molded by hands unseen yet near.
With time and warmth, we find our view,
Emerging stronger, shedding fear.

In solitude, the kiln does hum,
A rhythm of grinding and grace.
Through every heartbeat, we become,
A testament to love's embrace.

As seasons change, our hearts refine,
Forged in the fires of pain and hope.
With each pass, the spirit aligns,
In the journey, together we cope.

So let us trust in the process true,
With faith that the light has no end.
In the quiet kilns, we break through,
Emerging as seekers, souls to mend.

The Sacred Chronology of Souls

In the tapestry of life, we weave,
Threads of purpose interlace.
Every heartbeat, a dream we conceive,
In the divine, we find our place.

Time flows like a river vast,
Carrying whispers of those who've passed.
In sacred moments, shadows cast,
In loving memory, forever last.

As stars align, we gather near,
The echoes of ancestors guide our way.
In the silence, a voice we hear,
Connecting souls, night and day.

Through ages, the stories unfold,
In every soul, a legacy bright.
In compassion, we find the gold,
Binding together in love's pure light.

So let us honor the sacred time,
Each encounter a chance to grow.
In the chronology of souls so sublime,
We find our strength, love's eternal glow.

The Evolution of Our Purpose

In silence we seek, the whispers divine,
A journey of faith, where souls intertwine.
Each step that we take, a guiding embrace,
Illuminated paths, in this sacred space.

With hearts open wide, we gather as one,
United in love, our race has begun.
Evolving each day, in spirit and grace,
We find our true selves, in time and in place.

The tapestry woven, in colors so bright,
Threads of our purpose, we honor the light.
Through trials we rise, through shadows we stand,
Together as shepherds, of faith's gentle hand.

In moments of doubt, we turn to the skies,
With prayers as our anchor, our hearts will arise.
The lessons we learn, like seeds in the ground,
In the garden of hope, true peace can be found.

Our purpose unfolds, like flowers in bloom,
With wisdom of ages, dispelling the gloom.
In every heartbeat, a message so clear,
We dance in the light, casting out all fear.

The Promise of New Dawn

As night gives way, to the morning's embrace,
We gather our hearts, in a sacred space.
With promises whispered, as shadows depart,
A new day arising, igniting the heart.

Through valleys of struggle, where hope starts to fade,
We cling to the light, our spirits unafraid.
Each dawn brings renewal, a chance to believe,
In the promise of love, we are destined to weave.

The sun paints the sky, with hues of redemption,
A canvas of mercy, beyond comprehension.
From ashes we rise, like phoenixes strong,
With faith as our guide, we know we belong.

Let shadows be swallowed, by great beams of dawn,
In unity gathered, our fears will be gone.
For every heartbeat, a testament true,
In the promise of light, we are born anew.

So let us remember, when darkness is near,
The promise of dawn, forever is here.
In every new morn, we sing out in grace,
Together in joy, we find our true place.

A Covenant with The Future

In the stillness we stand, a promise embraced,
With hands joined together, our journeys interlaced.
A covenant forged, beneath heaven's gaze,
For the future awaits, in infinite ways.

With hearts full of courage, we venture ahead,
For the seeds of compassion, in harmony spread.
The whispers of hope, through ages resound,
In the tapestry woven, love's threads will be found.

We nurture the visions, with dreams that ignite,
Each soul a beacon, guiding through night.
In this covenant sacred, we promise to grow,
With wisdom and kindness, ever in tow.

A future is written, with ink of our grace,
A story of love, that time can't erase.
Through storms we may wander, yet strength we shall find,
In the unity cherished, our spirits aligned.

So let us embrace, this journey begun,
With hearts open wide, we rise like the sun.
A covenant guiding, where futures ignite,
In harmony blessed, we dance in the light.

The Testament of Our Growth

From the cradle of dawn, where dreams take their flight,
We rise like the sun, dispelling the night.
In every experience, a lesson bestowed,
The testament written, in paths that we strode.

With courage as armor, we weather the storm,
Through trials and triumphs, our spirits transform.
In the garden of life, our roots intertwine,
As blossoms of hope, with purpose align.

Each moment a gift, each heartbeat a prayer,
Reflecting the beauty, we find everywhere.
The trials we've faced, the victories too,
A testament strong, in all that we do.

We gather as one, a tapestry bold,
Stories of wisdom, in time to be told.
With love as our guide, we flourish and grow,
In the light of our truth, our essence we show.

The journeys we've traveled, they carve out our way,
In the testament written, our hearts shall not sway.
Together we blossom, through shadows and light,
In the growth of our souls, we find pure delight.

Milton Keynes UK
Ingram Content Group UK Ltd.
UKHW022223251124
451566UK00006B/100

9 789916 896730